a Rainbow of Animals

Literacy Consultant:
Allan A. De Fina, PhD
Dean, College of Education/Professor of Literacy
Education, New Jersey City University
Past President of the New Jersey Reading Association

Melissa Stewart

Science Consultant:
Helen Hess, PhD
Professor of Biology
College of the Atlantic
Bar Harbor, Maine

**northern
cardinal**

**leafy
sea dragon**

A Rainbow of Animals

panther chameleon

poison dart
frog

Go outside and look around. How many kinds of animals do you see? Snakes and birds are animals. So are spiders and insects.

Animals come in all sizes and shapes. And they come in all the colors of the rainbow.

leaf-mimic
katydid

purple emperor
butterfly

Red Animals Near You

Can you think of some red animals that live near you? Ladybugs are red. So are some birds and snakes.

Red animals live in other parts of the world, too. Let's take a look at some of them.

Scarlet Ibis

This bird is gray and white when it hatches from its egg. The chick eats lots of red crabs. This food changes the color of its feathers. By the time the bird is full grown, its body is bright red.

Bald Uakari

What do female uakaris (wah KAH rees) look for in a mate? A very red face. It means the male monkey is healthy, and he will make a good father.

Northern Cardinal

This male's bright colors send the same kind of message. They tell females he is strong and healthy. He will do a good job protecting the nest. And he will find lots of food for their chicks.

Great Frigate Bird

This bird's feathers are not red. But he still knows how to attract a female. He pumps air into a red pouch on his throat. Females can see it from far away.

Coral Snake

This snake's red rings send out a different message. They say, "Stay away!" If a predator gets too close, the snake will give it a painful bite full of poison.

Morpho Caterpillars

These caterpillars do not need to hide. They stay in a group instead. That makes them look like one large red creature. Most hungry birds will not go near them.

Pacific Giant Octopus

What does this octopus do when it spots an enemy? It changes its skin color to blend in with the rocks nearby.

Mandrill

Mandrills live in thick, dark forests. How do these monkeys find one another? They look for the bright red noses of their friends and family.

Where Do These Red Animals Live?

KEY: The orange areas on each map show where that animal lives.

Found on islands within this range

Orange Animals Near You

Can you think of some orange animals that live near you? Monarch butterflies are orange.

Orange animals live in other parts of the world, too. Let's take a look at some of them.

Bengal Tiger

Being orange helps some animals hide. This tiger's orange fur and black stripes make it hard to see. It can sneak through the grass and catch its prey by surprise.

Coral Grouper

A bright orange fish could really stand out. But not when it swims in front of a bright orange fan coral. Blending in helps animals stay safe. That is why many colorful creatures live on colorful coral reefs.

Scarab Beetle

Some land animals use the same kind of trick. This beetle is hard to see when it rests on an orange flower. That keeps it safe from birds, bats, and other predators.

Viceroy Butterfly

Some orange animals are easy to spot. Their bright colors send a message. They say, "Stay away!" After just one bite, a hungry bird spits this butterfly out. Yuck! It tastes bad.

Golden Mantella Frog

Most orange frogs taste bad, too. This keeps predators away. But this orange frog does *NOT* taste bad. Its color fools predators. They leave the frog alone.

Cock-of-the-Rock

This bird's orange feathers help him attract a mate. They say, "Look at me!" The female's body is not as bright. That helps her hide from predators while she sits on her eggs.

Panther Chameleon

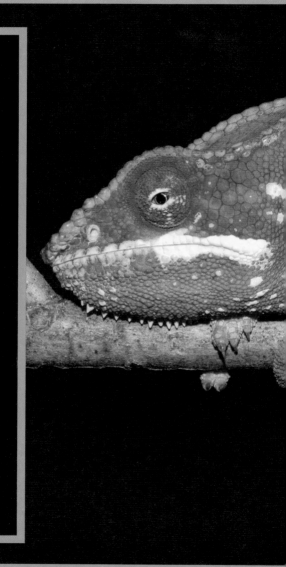

Most of the time, this lizard stays green. That helps it blend in with its forest home. But it can change its color when it wants to send a message. Sometimes it is trying to attract a mate. And sometimes it is telling other lizards to stay away.

Stinkbug

The bright colors of a stinkbug warn predators to stay away. If an enemy attacks, it will be sorry. The little insect will let out a nasty smell.

Where Do These Orange Animals Live?

KEY: The orange areas on each map show where that animal lives.

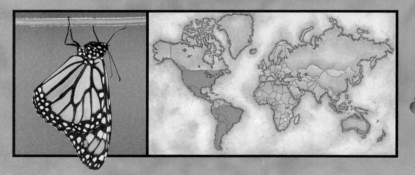

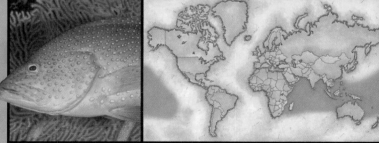

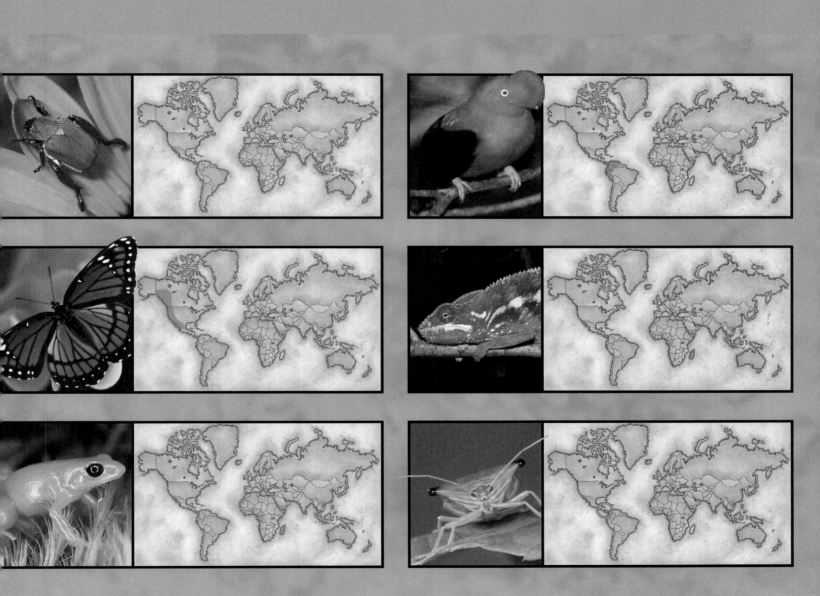

Yellow Animals Near You

Can you think of some yellow animals that live near you? Tiger swallowtail butterflies are yellow.

Yellow animals live in other parts of the world, too. Let's take a look at some of them.

Cup Moth Caterpillars

Some yellow animals are easy to spot. Their bright colors say, "Stay away!" If a hungry bird grabs one of these caterpillars, it will be sorry. The caterpillar's yellow spines give a painful sting.

Fire Salamander

This animal's bright colors send the same message. They tell enemies that the salamander's skin is full of poison. If an animal bites the salamander, it starts to feel sick. It drops the prey and leaves it alone.

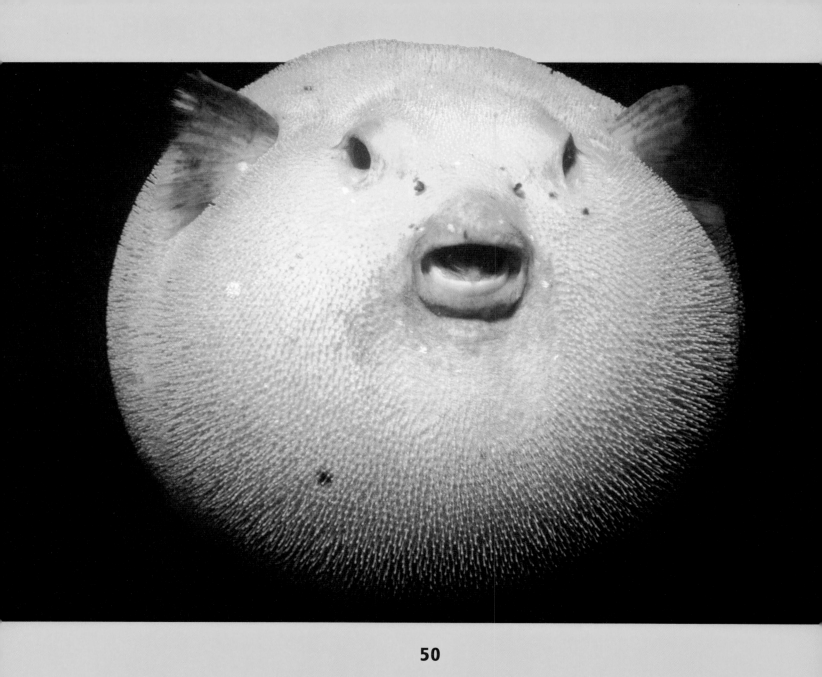

Guineafowl Pufferfish

This fish's bright colors do not always scare enemies. But the fish has another trick for staying safe. If an enemy gets too close, the fish blows up like a balloon. That makes it hard to bite.

Honeybee

A bee's black and yellow stripes say, "Stay away." If a bee feels scared, it stabs its enemy with its stinger. Ouch! That hurts! Poison in the stinger makes skin swell and itch.

American Goldfinch

Some animals want to send out a different message. Their yellow bodies say, "Come to me!"

In summer, a male goldfinch has bright yellow feathers. They help him attract a mate. In winter, he gets new feathers. They are brown to blend in with his grassy home.

African Lion

Being yellow helps some animals hide. When a lion lies down in the yellow grass, its yellow fur makes it hard to see. This helps it catch prey by surprise.

Leafy Sea Dragon

This is not a clump of seaweed. It is a fish. But its yellow color and leaf-like shape fool most predators. A leafy sea dragon floats most of the time. But it can turn using tiny fins on its head.

Great Horned Owl

It can be hard to see in the middle of the night. But light from the moon and stars bounces off the yellow part of this owl's eyes. That makes it easier for the owl to spot rabbits, mice, and other prey.

Eyelash Viper

An eyelash viper lives in deep, dark rain forests. But its bright colors can still help it hide from enemies. This viper blends in with the yellow fruits in a tree.

Where Do These Yellow Animals Live?

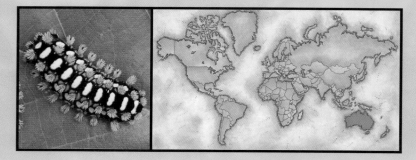

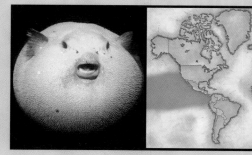

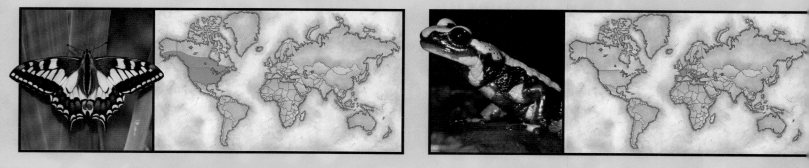

Green Animals Near You

Can you think of some green animals that live near you? A praying mantis is green.

Green animals live in other parts of the world, too. Let's take a look at some of them.

Leaf-Mimic Katydid

Small animals have many enemies. Their body colors often help them stay safe.

This little green insect looks like a leaf. Its shape and color help it blend in with its forest home.

Masked Puddle Frog

Animals cannot watch for danger when they are asleep. When this little frog feels tired, it curls up inside a leaf. The frog's green skin matches the leaf. That helps it stay safe while it takes a nap.

Yellow-Crowned Parrot

This parrot lives in tropical rain forests. Its green feathers make it hard to spot. When two of these birds need to find each other, they make loud calls. Then they fly toward the sound.

Green Anole Lizard

Most of the time, this lizard stays green. That helps it blend in with its forest home. But when an anole is worried or angry, it turns brown. The color change sends a message. It tells other lizards to stay away.

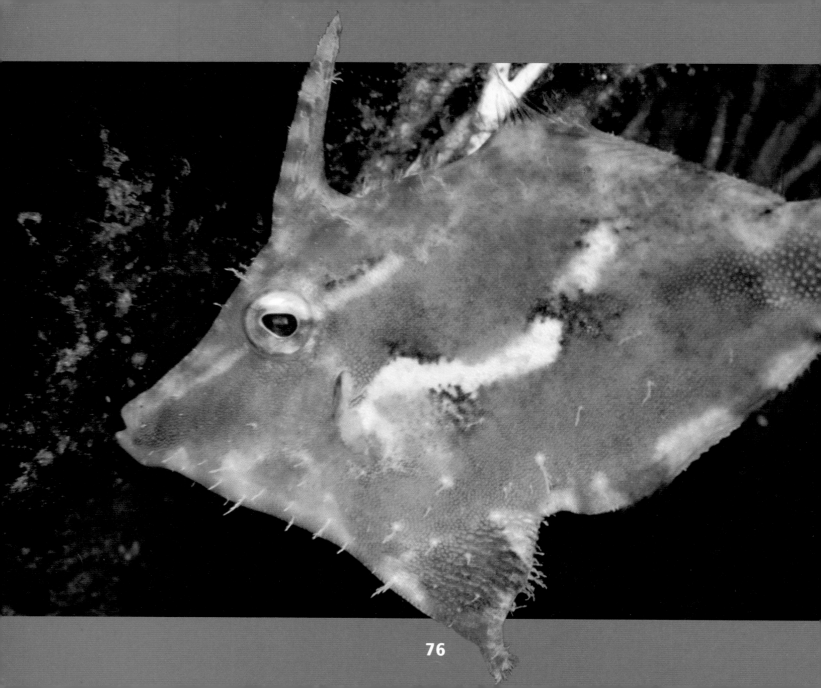

Diamond Leatherjacket Fish

This fish has a trick for staying safe. Its body looks just like the green algae it swims through all day long. When hungry predators pass by, they do not notice the little fish. It blends in with its home.

Brown-Throated Three-Toed Sloth

Algae often grow on a sloth's shaggy fur. During the day, these animals hang from trees and sleep. The green algae help the sloths blend in with their forest home, so hungry wild cats cannot spot them.

Mallard Duck

Sometimes being green helps an animal stand out. A male mallard's green head is easy to see. It helps him attract a mate. A female mallard has a brown head. It helps her hide from enemies while she sits on her nest.

Emerald Tree Boa

The emerald tree boa's colors help it hide from enemies. The colors also help this snake sneak up on animals to eat.

Where Do These Green Animals Live?

KEY:
The orange areas on each map show where that animal lives.

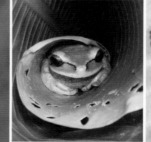

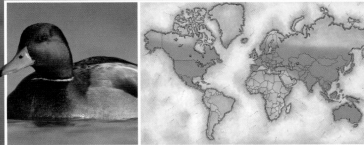

85

Blue Animals Near You

Can you think of some blue animals that live near you? A great blue heron is blue.

Blue animals live in other parts of the world, too. Let's take a look at some of them.

Blue Shark

Being blue helps some animals hide. This shark's blue body makes it hard to see as it swims through the ocean. That helps the hungry hunter sneak up on its prey.

Blue-Ringed Octopus

This animal's pale skin and blue rings make it stand out. When enemies see these bright colors, they know to stay away.

It would be a bad idea to attack this octopus. Its body has enough poison to kill twenty people.

Blue Poison Dart Frog

This little frog is easy to spot. But most predators will not try to eat it. The frog's bright colors say, "Watch out! I'm full of poison."

Indigo Bunting

Some animals want to send out a different message. Their blue bodies say, "Come to me!" This bird's bright feathers help him attract a mate. The female's feathers are light brown. They help her hide from predators.

Blue-Footed Boobies

At mating time, these birds put on an amazing show. The male spreads his wings wide and whistles. Then he struts, slides, shuffles, and stomps his bright blue feet. That's one good way to get a female to look at him!

Golden Monkeys

These monkeys live in mountain forests. Their light brown fur makes them hard to spot. Luckily, they know how to find one another. They just look for the bright blue faces of their family and friends.

Morpho Butterfly

The tops of this butterfly's wings really stand out, but the bottoms are light brown. When the insect rests with its wings folded up, it is very hard to see. If a predator gets too close, the butterfly snaps its wings open. The blue flash surprises the predator. That gives the butterfly a chance to get away.

Blue-Tongued Skink

This lizard has its own trick for staying safe. When an enemy attacks, the lizard sticks out its tongue. The bright color helps scare off the predator.

Blue Darner Dragonfly

This insect can change the color of its body. On cool mornings, it is dark blue. That helps its body warm up faster in the sun. On hot afternoons, the dragonfly turns light blue. That helps its body cool off.

Where Do These Blue Animals Live?

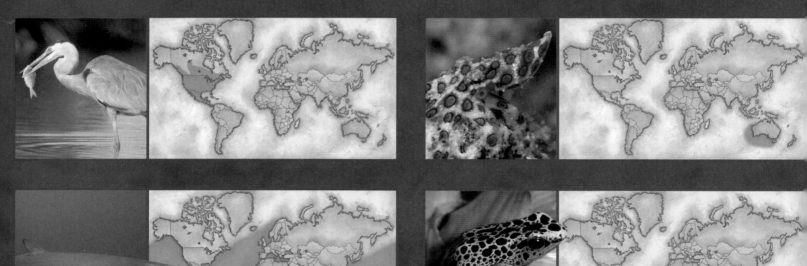

purple martins with two tree swallows

Purple Animals Near You

Can you think of some purple animals that live near you? Purple martin birds are purple.

Purple animals live in other parts of the world, too. Let's take a look at some of them.

Coralline Sculpin

This fish lives in places where purple, plantlike creatures grow on the ocean floor. That helps it blend in. It hides from larger fish that might want to eat it.

Crab Spider

This spider hunts smaller insects and spiders. It has no trouble catching its prey by surprise. It can turn yellow, purple, orange, pink, or white. That way it always matches the flower it is on. Prey cannot see it.

Crowned Wood Nymph

Sometimes being purple helps an animal stand out. This bird's bright body is easy to spot. It helps him attract a mate. The female's feathers are green. That helps her blend in with nearby leaves.

Purple Emperor Butterfly

This male butterfly's bright body sends a message to other males. It says, "Stay away. This is my home." The other males know they need to find somewhere else to live.

Agama Lizard

Most lizards live alone, but this male is part of a large group of lizards. His colorful skin lets the other lizards know that he is the boss.

Nudibranch

    This sea slug lives in the ocean. It may be small, but it is easy to spot. Its bright colors say, "Leave me alone." If a hungry hunter takes a bite, it will be sorry. A sea slug's body is full of poison.

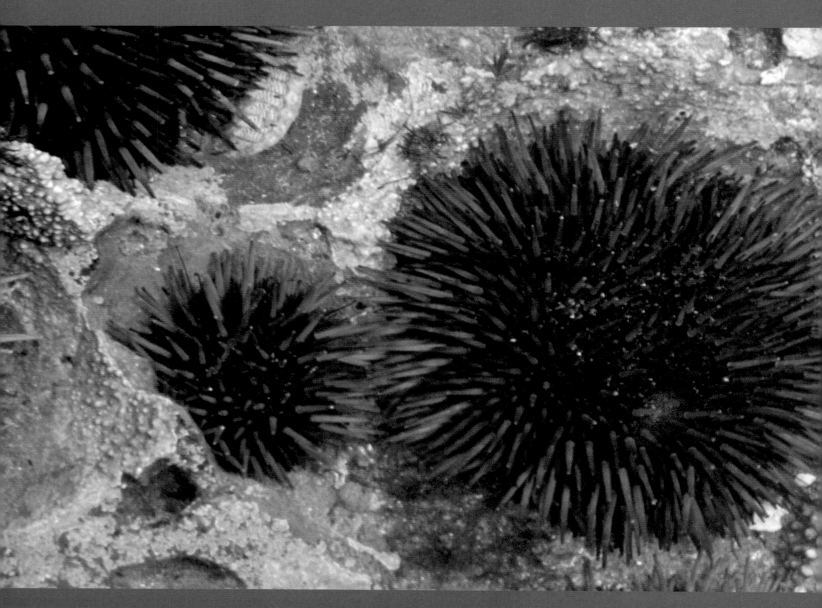

Purple Sea Urchins

Sea urchins make a tasty treat for some ocean animals. But most do not go near them. Predators know that a sea urchin's long spines give a painful prick.

Fungus Beetle

The purple body of a fungus beetle warns predators to stay away. If an enemy attacks, it will be sorry. The little insect will let out a bad smell.

Where Do These Purple Animals Live?

KEY:
The orange areas on each map show where that animal lives.

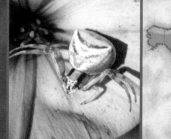

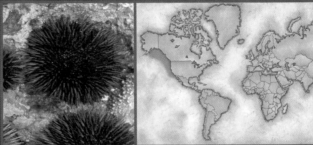

More Colorful Animals

Animal Colors: <http://www.highlightskids.com> *Then type* Animal Colors *in the search box.*

Camouflage Game: <http://www.abc.net.au> *Then type* Camouflage Game *in the search box.*

Enslow Elementary, an imprint of Enslow Publishers, Inc.

Enslow Elementary® is a registered trademark of Enslow Publishers, Inc.

Copyright © 2010 by Melissa Stewart

Library of Congress Cataloging-in-Publication Data

Stewart, Melissa.
   A rainbow of animals / Melissa Stewart.
      p. cm.
   Includes bibliographical references.
   Summary: "Explains why animals come in each color of the rainbow using examples of animals in the wild"—Provided by publisher.
   ISBN 978-0-7660-3706-9
   1. Animals—Color—Juvenile literature. I. Title.
   QL767.S744 2010
   591.47'2—dc22
                                                            2009036706

Printed in the United States of America

112009 Lake Book Manufacturing, Inc., Melrose Park, IL

10 9 8 7 6 5 4 3 2 1

To Our Readers: We have done our best to make sure all Internet Addresses in this book were active and appropriate when we went to press. However, the author and the publisher have no control over and assume no liability for the material available on those Internet sites or on other Web sites they may link to. Any comments or suggestions can be sent by e-mail to comments@enslow.com or to the address on the back cover.

♻ Enslow Publishers, Inc., is committed to printing our books on recycled paper. The paper in every book contains 10% to 30% post-consumer waste (PCW). Our goal is to do our part to help young people and the environment too!

Photo Credits: Minden Pictures: © Adrian Davies/npl, pp. 44–45, 64; © Barry Mansell/npl, p. 3; © Birgitte Wilms, pp. 76–77, 85, 90–91, 106; © Brent Hedges/npl, pp. 2, 58–59, 65; © Cisca Castelijns/Foto Natura, pp. 66–67, 84; © Claus Meyer, pp. 8–9, 22; © Cyril Ruoso/JH Editorial, pp. 20–21, 23; © David Tipling/npl, pp. 36–37, 43; © Eddy Marissen/Foto Natura, pp. 1 (bottom left), 122–123, 127; © Fred Bavendam, pp. 18–19, 23, 28–29, 42, 50–51, 64; © Gerry Ellis, pp. 32–33, 43, 56–57, 65, 74–75, 82–83, 85; © Greg Harold/Auscape, pp. 102–103, 107; © Hans Cristoph Kappel/npl, pp. 3, 116–117, 127; © Ingo Arndt/Foto Natura, pp. 1 (top center), 40–41, 46–47, 64, 101 (inset); © Konrad Wothe, pp. 4–5, 22, 52–53, 65, 72–73, 85, 112–113, 126; © Marcel van Kammen, pp. 80–81, 85; © Martin Harvey/Foto Natura, pp. 34–35, 43; © Michael & Patricia Fogden, pp. 1 (top right, bottom right, and bottom center), 14–15, 23, 30–31, 43, 62–63, 65, 70–71, 78–79, 84, 85, 92–93, 100–101, 106, 107, 114–115, 124–125, 127; © Michael Durham, pp. 60–61, 65; © Mitsuaki Iwago, pp. 26–27, 42; © Norbert Wu, pp. 24–25, 88–89, 106, 120–121, 127; © Pete Oxford, pp. 2, 38–39, 43; © Piotr Naskrecki, pp. 3, 68–69, 84; © Rene Krekels/Foto Natura, pp. 48–49, 64; © Rod Williams/npl, pp. 1 (top left), 6–7, 22; © Rolf Nussbaumer/npl, p. 42; © S & D & K Maslowski/FLPA, pp. 54–55, 65; © Tim Fitzharris, pp. 104–105, 107; © Tom Vezo, pp. 2, 10–11, 23, 94–95, 107, 108–109, 126; © Tui De Roy, pp. 12–13, 23, 86–87, 96–97, 106, 107; © ZSSD, pp. 98–99, 107.
Naturepl.com: © Bernard Castelein, pp. 118–119, 127; © Jeff Rotman, pp. 110–111, 126; © Luiz Claudio Marigo, pp. 16–17, 23.

Map Credits: © 1999, Artville, LLC, pp. 22–23, 42–43, 64–65, 84–85, 106–107, 126–127.

Cover Photographs: Minden Pictures (front cover, clockwise from top left): © Rod Williams/npl; © Ingo Arndt/Foto Natura; © Michael & Patricia Fogden (top right, bottom right, and bottom center); Eddy Marissen/Foto Natura; (back cover): © Tom Vezo (bird); © Martin Harvery/Foto Natura (frog).

Enslow Elementary
an imprint of
Enslow Publishers, Inc.
40 Industrial Road
Box 398
Berkeley Heights, NJ 07922
USA

http://www.enslow.com